THE VOICE OF THE OCEAN

THE VOICE OF THE OCEAN

BY

WILLIAM HOPE HODGSON

WILDSIDE PRESS

First printed . . . 1921

Almost indeed
  I wish I now were dead
    Could I but shine some light
  Along the path I sped,
    To cheer the stumbling hearts
          across the night,
A light to souls in need.
              W.H.H.

THE VOICE OF THE OCEAN

Upon one clear, cool day, when little winds
Played a soft chime upon the ocean's bells,
Passed a great steamer on its way from shore
Bearing to far off lands a multitude
Of the small souls which form the staple part
Of this old world's inhabitants.   And they,
To pass the time away, with much small talk
Skimmed o'er the surface of the Sea of Thought,
Having no thought of drowning in its depths
Through very lack of knowledge that 'twas deep.

Said one of highest breed and leanest brain :—

" 'Tis foolishness this vain belief in God,
Who is He ?—No one knows, nor ever will ;
He is but Something born within the minds
Of mankind in the mass—WE know too well
How empty is such thought ; and, knowing this,
We live our lives content , for soon the end
Shall come, and we shall be no more at all."

Thus ended he.   The woman smiled, to whom
He had thus posed as a philosopher ;
Then simpered on from God to talk of dress.
   But lo ! from all the sea a murmur rose,
Impressive to the wise because it held
Meaning beyond the common words of man :
Yet those upon the deck took little heed ;
They knew it not ; but thought it was the wind
Mournful among the waves.   And so they passed.
   Yet I, who had been wise through dying soon,
Heard and interpreted, and this it was :—

   " I have seen God !   And who are ye who say,
With such assurance, that there is no God ?
Again, I ask, Who are ye, and from whence ?
And asking, laugh your littleness to scorn,
For even your beginnings are not known
To ye, O small and febrile things, who flash
In one short instant through your small gamut
Of feelings insignificant, and whose
Whole life and knowledge are no more than breath,
Measured according to my pulsing heart !
   " Did ye then live in those unknown, strange days,
When God and I conversed, and He, abroad
Upon my seething waters, spoke of you,
As of some things that were to come at last,

8

THE VOICE OF THE OCEAN

In some dim future time when this round world
Was fitted for ye by the hands of Time ? "

   The voice was quiet a moment ; then again
It hushed to silence every tinkling wave,
And thus it spoke :—

      " Listen, and ye shall learn !—
In the abyss of time, when God was young,
When heaven was one void of holy light,
When the great stars slept in the future's womb,
And human atoms were undreamt of dust,
There swept from far beyond time's spaceless sea
A sound of thunder—'twas the voice of God,
And at the sound the solemn light was gapped,
Dark streakings fled across it, and there grew,
Amid the calmer light, clots of hot fire,
As light drew unto light—rotating flames,
As the pale light of heav'n massed into shapes—
The nebula of unformed suns, and grew
Smaller, by aeons, casting off loose worlds,
Their flaming children, which in turn gave birth
To lesser worlds of fire, and so was born
The universe of suns and worlds, of which
This fireless world is part, as is one grain
Of sand a portion of some mighty waste.
   " Ages passed on ; then was I born to life,

THE VOICE OF THE OCEAN

Born into life with the hot blood of fire,
Floating with thunders on the breath of flames.
  " In infancy and childhood, wrapped in steam,
I slept through centuries, anon disturbed
With the fierce tumult by my passions wrought,
Till after many ages I awoke
And looked around upon a world of war,
Where great volcanoes—torches for the gods,
Lit the black dome which canopied the world.
  " Aeons fled onward whilst I fought and learnt,
And so I came to know of God till we
Talked many an age of years—He teaching me
From the surrounding chaos of the world
Dread lessons writ in storms and roaring fires
Till, somewhat, I perceived the mighty sense
Speaking within the tumult of the earth—
Shouting of life on life, of things beyond
My youthful intellect and younger heart,
Teaching the waiting lesson ; so at last
Was I prepared to bear my wondrous task.
  " The world had sunk to quietness ere I knew
The full import of that which ailed in me :
I scarce could rest in peace, so strange I felt.
  " Pregnant I was—uneasy in my calm,
Until my time was full for giving birth ;
Then, 'mid the shakings of a mighty storm,
I lay convulsed in agony, while winds

THE VOICE OF THE OCEAN

Screamed in terrific unison.   On high
God looked down on to me all sorrowing,
And all unable to give help or ease.
So through tremendous years of pain, my voice
Shouted my grief across a quaking sky,
So that the unavailing winds, all drowned
Within that star-loud, reverberating sound,
Seemed but as gentle whispers—purling streams
Blent in the roar of some stupendous fall.
And lo ! when it was o'er, around my breasts,
White with the foamy milk of life, there lay
Upon my midnight waters, vastly grim,
Ten-thousand times ten-thousand souls new born,
Like scarcely fallen snow-flakes on dark rocks.
   " Thus was creation now achieved, and so,
In his right time, man was evolved, and grew
Into his present shape, with underneath
His heavier flesh, a soul such as was born
In that supremely distant time, when man,
As ye now know him, was undreamt of earth ! "

   Some hours of silence followed, while the Sea
Rested, as though communing with itself,
Till, in the West, the night soared up on wings
Of gorgeous colours, that too soon were grey.
   Then, as the dark came down upon the Sea,
Strange voices called from the surrounding air—

Sadness and want spoke chiefly in their tones,
Though all were not thus, as thou soon shalt hear.

Then from the Sea a whisper rose, and said :—

" Hark ye, these be the souls of those who sleep,
Perchance, in distant countries, while their minds
Steal out across my waters seeking rest,
Or wisdom.   Yet when they awake have they
No knowledge nor remembrance, save it be
Something of which they think as dim-lit dreams."

From the surrounding voices one broke clear,
Despair and doubt in every tone it seemed :—

" Thou Bodyless Thing in the sky,
    Wherefore am I ?
      For why so alone ?
        Ah !   Master of Death,
        For why this mad breath ?
          Which Thou could'st allay,
          Nor lengthen my stay
Upon this drear planet of stone."

'Twas thus the Sea replied :—

            " Thou art alone
Because by loneliness thou shalt be taught

The hideous solitude which Sin doth cast
About the soul.   Thy present loneliness
May serve to save thy soul from future woe ;
So bear it as thou canst.

                " As for thy breath,
Learn now to temper thy hot soul with strength
From the surrounding air.   Curtail all vice,
And work to strengthen that which was thy will,
Thus may this stony planet prove a joy,
Because upon it thou shalt work, through hope,
To further knowledge and the joy of peace.

  " Thou askest why thou art.   I cannot tell,
Save that it be God's Will ; and only He
In the whole breadth of space can answer thee.

  " Now pass thee on with mind intent to live
So that thou shalt attain to peace at last."

  Scarcely had the Sea finished when I heard,
From the encircling silence, one sad voice :—

    " O, Sea, I have been lonely
      For years afar from thee !
        Dumb 'mid an earless People, I strove to
          speech, in vain.
        I had been better served had I
        But held my peace as life passed by,
      And silent borne my pain !

THE VOICE OF THE OCEAN

" I spoke about God's bounty,
    But sneers were all my gain ;
      I held out hope with both my hands ;
      I sang of God's glad Wonder-Lands,
    Yet it was all in vain ! "

It ceased, and through the stillness that befell
The Sea made answer so my soul was glad :—

    " To only the unthinking mind appears
      The thought that he who casts himself on spears
      Has failed. I tell you he has won
      The highest prize ; I care not where he aimed !
      For, you must know, 'tis *he* who leads the
          van—
    Weak souls may *follow* after one such man ! "

  In the succeeding quietness, low I caught
A quick, sweet sob of gladness, and I knew
That one beweighted heart within the world
Was saved from failure's burden. While great Hope
Thrilled in the soul of one who had been sore ;
Revivifying faith to greater life.

  And now the voice of one a-dying crept
Sadly across the night to me. It seemed
Full of a sadness, past all comforting :—

THE VOICE OF THE OCEAN

" Must it be adieu, O, Sea,
   Must it be adieu ?
The very thought is pain to me,
   Yet, from thy quivering blue,
      I seem to hear thy sad assent,
For whispers come from thee,
   (Soft as the weeping of the dew,
      Like sorrowing voices sadly blent,)
Telling that it must be——"

The voice trailed off to silence, and the Sea
Thus made reply in a most saddened voice :—

" Full well I share thy grief—To-morrow's dawn
Shall steal across my breast and find thee not :
O, bitter are all partings !   Yet they serve
But to enhance our love.   Pray thou to God
That we shall meet some other time, elsewhere,
If not upon this world.
                    " Now comfort thee !
And fear not death ; it is thy greatest friend,
Its pain is but the birth to fuller life,
And after that again to life more vast,
Until thou hast attained to the Last Life.
Where thou shalt breathe deep life beyond belief.
   Ah ! now good-bye—good-bye !   God grant thee
      speed

Through the strange birth of death—through all thy
    deaths ! "

Sadly an answer wailed across the Sea :—

" When I am dead, O, Sea,
    As a strange mist upon thy breast
Shall I float back to thee,
    Out from the great and dark unrest
Of all eternity ! "

The Sea's voice, singing sadly, then replied :—

" Dear piteous soul,
    Be comforted !
    When thou art dead
(Though multitudes of ages roll)
      My old, sad heart
        Shall dream of thee,
      Who feeleth now death's bitter smart ;
        And if thou should'st come back to me
          How gladly would my billows cry
        Their joy to thee
          Who art about to die !

" Be comforted ! Be comforted !
    When thou art dead,

THE VOICE OF THE OCEAN

I shall still dream of thee
When thou hast long forgotten me ! ”

In sadness and in doubt now spoke the soul :—

" After my death, if all alone I tread
My ghostly way along thy lonely coasts,
Wilt thou still know me ? Or shall I be lost
Unto thy sight, and seem no more than mist
Floating upon thy fringe, hair dipt in spume ? ”

In deep emotion spoke the Sea thuswise :—

" Thou who dost love me so, I cannot tell,
Save that it seems to me thy very love
Shall show thy soul to me amid the mists :
Then shall I take thee to my heart till thou
Art comforted enough to go to God.
  " Ah ! then, indeed, thou shalt begin to learn
That love as mine and thine is cold as death,
Beside the passion that God has for souls ! ”

The Ocean ceased from speaking, and the soul
Slid down upon the Sea to rest, while far
From some benighted land a sound of bells,
Ringing a solemn knell, told of some death ;
And the vast Sea in sympathy replied

With the deep beatings of its mighty heart.
  And from far down a sound of singing rose,
As though a wondrous requiem were sung—
A requiem full of sadness ; but with hope
Sounding most splendidly among its notes.
  A certain time passed on, and then a voice
From some long distant shore came o'er the Sea
Most hopeless in its sadness. And it seemed
It moaned in hollow notes this epitaph :—

    " Sleep thou in thy bed of clay,
       In that darkness where no light
          Comes to wake thee from thy rest,
       Comes to wake thy lasting night :
    Shut from gleam of earthly day
       Slumber on, for so 'tis best !

    " One brief moment it may seem
       Ere a trumpet's note shall sound,
       And thy rested soul shall rise
      From its bed of clay embound,
    From that long and silent dream
       To a Judgment in the skies."

Somewhat impatient, then exclaimed the Sea :—

" Much nonsense is contained within such lines !
There is no need for judgment. Thou shalt live

THE VOICE OF THE OCEAN

In many lives among thy deeds until
Thou shalt attain to the Last Life.   How then
Shalt thou need judging when thou art involved.
For evermore in all that thou hast worked,
Both good and harmful ?

        " Nay, there is no need
Of judgment ; for thou mightest quite as well
Talk of such things to one who has prepared
A bed of holly thorns on which to sleep,
His punishment's assured.   Leave him alone !

  " Likewise, hath one prepared a couch of peace,
There is no need for judgment.   He is sure
Of a most joyous sleep.   Leave him alone !

  " Thus art thou making to thyself a bed,
For all eternity, compact of deeds,
On which to lie.   And whether, or not, thy rest
Be peaceful doth depend upon thyself !

  " Thou weavest thine own shroud, or thine own
    robe,
The death of joy, or greater bliss of life.

  " 'Tis all a matter for thine own concern,
For thou thyself must suffer thine own harm ;
Likewise, enjoy all good that thou hast worked
Throughout all time.

       " So, truly, shalt thou learn
That thine own deeds are thy remorseless judges ! "

THE VOICE OF THE OCEAN

Soul :—" O, Sea,
    I cannot e'er agree
    With thy strange teachings, which seem
      blasphemy
    To me ! "

Sea :— " Some judgment of the kind
    Thou holdest in thy mind.
      Why must
      Distrust
    Still torture humankind ? "

Soul :—" O, Sea,
    It seems to me
      All mankind shall be judged
        And weighed ;
        It shall not be delayed ;
        Nor past the book of sin
        Can any human win,
      Nor any record from its page be smudged ! "

Sea :—" O, soul,
    With pondering
    Upon the final goal—
      With much long wondering
      I tired, to slumbering,
        And in my sleep I dreamed

THE VOICE OF THE OCEAN

Thy Judgment Day had come
With its tremendous sum
Of threatened misery,
And this is how it seemed
As I lay sleepily——"

Soul :—" One moment, Sea !
Art speaking seriously ?
Thou speakest with such zest,
Methinks thou hast some jest
Lurking within thy breast ! "

The Sea spoke not awhile ; but rested, and began :—

" 'Twas in my dreams I heard a trumpet's note
Come ringing down the aisles of time in throbs—
The last, long bugle-call sound o'er the world,
A clang'rous, threatening bray that shivered through
And through my soul.
                    " My heart-beats seemed to cease
As from the heaving earth I saw drive up
The misty forms of long forgotten dead.
Forgotten now no longer, fast they came,
Piecemeal and limbless, dreadful in their shrouds ;
But growing every moment into shape
As flying limbs came jostling through the air
In anxious haste to take a rightful place.

" Thus, as I watched, came to them face and form ;
But lo ! unheard, unthought of thing, their clothes
Had failed to resurrect, and thus each one
Stood naked on the earth, while that bold sun
Looked down with brazen face upon it all,
And smiled, an awesome, wicked smile, as though
It all along had known, forseen that this
Should be ; that these poor dames and gentlemen
Should stand unclothed in punishment to see
Their manifold transgressions written large
Upon each others naked breasts ; so thus
Each man, each woman, knew the others worth
At once, for all time, in a single glance.

" I saw them look and then attempt to hide
Their nakedness.   No use !   They had no clothes !
And God looked grimly down from that white throne.

" Then, like a thunder-peal, His voice rang out
To those poor shiv'ring corpses :—
                              " ' Let the dead
Make haste their dead to bury from Mine eyes ;
For sure am I that this offends My sight ! '

" At once each wakeful corpse began to throw
The moist brown earth upon a neighbour's head,
And each, retaliating, cast it back,
Until a plain of heaving, rolling mould
Ran undulating where awhile before
Had stood those shame-faced corpses.   And above,

THE VOICE OF THE OCEAN

God smiled a stern and bitter smile as He
Watched their endeavour, all their pitiful toil
To hide each other from themselves and Him.
  " And yet, methought the sternness of His smile
Had something in it tender, as He grasped
The grim, pathetic humour of it all.
  " And then I waked, and knew it for a dream—
A dream to me—a nightmare to the world
Who swallow that which Reason doth reject."

The Sea ceased from its humour, and the soul,
Disgusted and abashed, now held its peace.

A little time passed by ; then was the night
Rent with the screamings of a frightened soul :—

  " O, Jesu, in the hour of death, I pray
To Thee, O Tender One, in my distress—
Save Thou my frightened soul from this cold grasp !
Receive me, O my Christ, in Thine embrace.
  " I cannot face these loathly terrors felt ;
I shrink from THIS ! My Jesu, hear my prayer ;
Turn not away ; O Christ, turn not away !
The fiend has me !—Jesu, my Christ, *assist !*
Thou would'st not leave me, Christ —No ! Jesu, No !
Think of the PIT, my Christ ! Think of the PIT !
The gaping, hideous PIT !- God save my soul

THE VOICE OF THE OCEAN

From this Vast Foulness! Spare me, O my God!
Thou canst not fail me, God above! I weep
In misery most abject, God of Love;
Yes, love *me*, SAVE ME!—God, Thou canst not fail!
In   Jesu's   name   I   ask   it—Thou   S–H–A–L–T
    hear!——
God!—— O God!!—— *THE PIT ! ! !* 'Tis opening
    wide
For   me,   Father,   My   God!——   Jesu,   My
    C–H–R–I–S–T——!
Jesu!—— Jesu! I'm————Oh! My God!————
G ————O ——————D ———————
————————————————————!"

    The voice died in one shriek. And silence reigned,
As though the very night, with pity, held
Its breath in sympathy for that poor soul
Deeming itself already doomed, ere death
Could prove to it that joy was not at end.
    Then, in soliloquy, the Sea's low voice
Sounded most solemnly across the dark—

      Rising, wailing, strange and solemn,
      Sad, inhuman—yet all loving,
      Trailing upward from the deep,
      Singing from a cold abyss,
      Crying from a clouded gloom :—

24

THE VOICE OF THE OCEAN

" O, that such fear exists doth sorrow me !
How dreadful is religion that doth teach
Such terror to an erring soul !
                    " E'en now
That soul, whose agony ye heard, has waked
To further life—to greater wisdom, and
To *hope renewed !*
                    " Dost think ye are condemned
Or ever ye have felt sweet wisdom's touch ?
O, nay ! nay !   God worketh not thuswise—
    " True ! ye shall not escape your wrongful deeds ;
But He doth mean ye shall have had fair chance
To win to joy, ere ye reach the Last Life.
    " How think ye, born in ignorance as *this,*
God (Justice) would allow ye to be doomed
To joyless aeons of actual agony,
Without good chance to win to aeons of joy ?
    " O, nay ! though your wrong deeds shall punish ye,
I tell ye, once again, ye shall have chance
To win from grief in newer, greater lives,
With wisdom in your brains, peace in your hearts,
Growing from present seed to magnitude
Beyond belief in this first stage of life
Where ignorance doth flourish for a time."

A further space passed by, and then there came
A voice exalted with the wine of sin,

A woman's voice it was ; thuswise it ran :—
 " Not even Thou, O God, canst rob
 From me this hour of earthly joy,
 And afterwards, Thou may'st destroy
 My very soul—I care no jot
 If in Thy Hell I lie and rot !
 O'er sin itself I ride above
 Upon the splendour of my love——! "

 It ended suddenly as if 'twere checked
By retributive Right. Then spake the Sea
In a sad, thoughtful voice which seemed to pierce
To Reason's very deep, and echo there
From its cold bottom to the topmost skies :—

 " Poor child ! Hast thou e'er thought upon thy death
As a cessation from the joys of earth ?
Then know that every death thou diest leads on
To a much fuller life, including all
That thou hast thought and lived in those before.
And as a fuller life implies more power
To live, to understand, to suffer pain,
So may'st thou comprehend that on each life
Shall stand thy cause to suffer pain or joy
When the Last Life be reached, and thou shalt live
In culmination of all joy and grief
That thou hast ever known in all thy lives.
 " Pass on, pass on. I would not chide at all ;

But warn thee and direct, so that thou shalt,
In the Last Life, have no sad cause to wail
O'er wanton moments birthing aeons of pain."

Then from the rounding spirits one spoke out
In the thin tone of age—an old man's voice :—

" Ah ! would I could attain back to my youth
When but to live was to be praising God !
Odd times I get some whiff of that old joy ;
Within the scent of roses it steals back—
The old delicious smell of happy youth,
And then it drifts away, and I am left
Older, by contrast, than I was before.
" So when church bells come pealing softly past
Over some grassy hill, within the dusk,
Doth the low pastoral sound fill me with peace
Brimming with echoes of my childhood's days.
" And then the dark ahead, that draweth near,
Comes down upon me like a blank dismay,
And I am filled with fears, and scarcely can
Believe in life past death ; for faith comes hard
When the tremendous moment is at hand."

Thus spake the Sea :—

                    " Be of good cheer, old man,
When thou art dead, time's space shall be thy road ;

THE VOICE OF THE OCEAN

Thou shalt pass back or forward as thou wilt.
To happiest moments of past lives, thy soul
May dart along time's road to old delights—
Living long ages in one pang of joy :
Thus thou shalt reach the days of childhood's joys.
And live there till thy soul hath grown at last
To a desire to taste the fuller zest
That waits on manhood in a greater life."

Scarce had the Sea grown silent when I heard
A voice come shrilly laughing o'er the sea :—

" Ha ! Ha !—Ha ! Ha !
Get Thee to Thy kingdom, God !
I laugh at Thee !
Thou threatenest with a rod
That doth not frighten me ;
What indeed's Thy Hell to me ?
God, I have no fear of Thee !
Heaven and Hell have never been,
Save within men's wildered minds,
Dazed by light which only blinds,
Nor art Thou, I truly ween !
Here I live as pleases me—
When I've lived as likes me best
I shall die and be at rest.

THE VOICE OF THE OCEAN

Hark !   O Phantom Deity !
Ha ! Ha !—Ha ! Ha ! "

The Sea's voice came in quietly.   Such contempt
I ne'er had dreamed existed.
                                        Thus it spake :—

" Dost know, poor thing, that, somewhere on time's
          plain,
Ten-thousand aeons hence thy cackling laugh
Shall sound to thy distress ?
                                        " O, Ignorance !
No deed shall die, nor has, nor ever can !
Each moment that has been, forever lives ;
Thou art now being born somewhere in time ;
Thy mother's pangs are still existent.   Thou
Art still essaying thy first breath on earth !
So each deed thou hast wrought still lives.   Thou art
E'en now (*and for all time*) most horribly
Intent upon the lowest deed that e'er
Thy brains and hands have worked to thy dishonour,
For God and all Immortals who may care
To watch thee.
                                " Ah ! poor thing !   When thou hast died
Thou shalt stand high above that plain, and watch,
Among the past, but living, hours, thyself
Doing such things as shall break thee with shame.

Ah ! then shalt surely learn that heaven and hell
Are made up of thy deeds of good and harm ;
For in the Last Life thou shalt greatly live
Amid all good and evil thou hast wrought !
 " E'en now thy life I see—a tiny track
Smudging time's plain with filth a little way,
And little scenes show clearly that do grieve
Most utterly my heart ; for thou hast filled
This life unto its brim with future griefs.
 " O, if thou could'st but understand this thing,
That back within time's space eternally,
Before and after death, and all the while,
Thy deeds are still enacted—good and bad !
 " Do thou but wander back along time's road
Thou shalt come to the years of bygone lives,
And see thyself in sickly ignorance
Working the woeful deeds thou now dost work.
 " Poor soul ! Spite of contempt, I feel within,
For thee, more pity than thou can'st conceive,
Thou hast laid up such sorrow for thyself ! "

 Now, from above, there crept a moaning sound,
As though one spoke among the distant stars ;
Awhile I waited till the words were clear,
And thus :—

 " Quiet, O ye heavens while we speak !
God of all gods, through the eternal night,

Loaded with dead, we march enwrapped in gloom ;
Ten-thousand ages gone we rode in life,
Strong with the germ that lives where'er is light,
And bearing on a myriad life, where death
Played its sad havoc to exterminate
But all in vain ; for from our mighty hearts
Pulsed a life-stream which death could not subdue.
Yet, by Thy will, because of length of days,
Our time drew near for death.   Our blazing suns
Gave but a saddening light which dwindled on
From red to deeper red, until in gloom
We sank into vast graves of all that had
Lived on our bosoms in the days of light.
    " This have we borne, O God, but in the hope
That Thou would'st succour us to further life ;
Else if we thus must die with all our souls,
What use hath been our life ?   'Twere better far
We had not lived at all, than come to this—
Dark, hideous bulks of death within the void !
    " O God, if Thou art, as we have believed,
Almighty past our power to understand,
Then shalt Thou give us further life, or Thou
Art but abusing Thine Almighty Strength ! "

    Then spake the Sea :—·

                    " Patience, thou deathly worlds !
God's Might is right, because that self-same Might

THE VOICE OF THE OCEAN

Is governed and directed by a Mind
Born of the awful strength which lives in God.
And as a Mind so born and so sustained
Must be of breadth and height beyond finite,
So doth God justice where the finite mind
Would fail contemptibly to mete out right ;
Using its puny mind and puny strength
Unwittingly to forward some abuse,
Because of insufficient might to reach
To heights where justice may be dealt out pure.
   " Now have thou patience, for no mind can guess
What the vast womb of time may hold concealed ;
Yet of one thing thou may'st well be assured,
That all development is worked through change ;
So dies the corn ere born to further life,
One ear to life an hundred times as great ;
So may'st thou live again, for bear in mind
That in the furthest limit of all space
A lonely universe of silent worlds,
Dead aeons before thou had'st been nebula,
May on some orbit vast be nearing thee,
Though half eternity should pass ere they
Meet thee in full career. Ah ! then the skies
Shall witness thy new birth, as in one bound
Dead world shall leap unto dead world, and each
Shall flash from death to life within one breath—
To life for some long age of mightier life,

THE VOICE OF THE OCEAN

Tremendous in one flame as new as love.
" Bear this in mind to help thee through the aeons,
And know thou all the while within thy soul
That the last sorrows of ten-thousand worlds
Are stored within the tender heart of God."

The Sea then ceased from speaking, and a voice,
Of one who would talk boastful, sounded loud :—

" Wondrous is God.   But, surely, as all good
Springeth from His deep heart, so none may doubt
(If He be the Creator of all things)
Likewise, that from His breast all evil floats,
Pervading this whole world.   For He is proud,
And when He stumbles none may put Him right,
Nor whisper in His winds reproveful words,
Wherefore should He condemn us when we fall ? "

The question now propounded, did the voice
Stop with a foolish triumph in its tone,
At which the Sea grew angry, and fierce words
Leapt through the mad white welter of quick waves,
As its abysmal voice cried out with rage
Throughout the reeking sky, while over all
Flashed fitfully the cold, stern light of storms :—

" O trenchant fool !   And if thou provest this

THE VOICE OF THE OCEAN

What step hast thou advanced along the road
To further peace ?   Thou hast no aim it seems,
But to teach lessons in an art of eggs,
Which, truth ! thou teachest badly.   Dost thou think
To judge God by such standard as thou would'st
Apply to beings finite ?   Get thee hence !
And know that thy whole genius is one spark
Blown from the shining suns which stud God's ring !
Would'st thou with thy one spark put God to rights ? "

    Thus spake the Sea, and calming from its rage,
Listened as some fresh soul cried out in doubt :—

    " My soul is filled with doubt ; I do not know
How to tell right from wrong ; I am confused !
To all religions have I turned for help.
    " Apart from creed, they tell me that I have
A sense called ' Conscience,' which shall surely lead
My soul apart from harm, do I but try
To follow out its warnings through my life.
    " Now this is strange to me ; I have found men
'Mong savage tribes who thought no wrong to slay,
But rather counted it as doing good,
Depending on some teaching of their creed.
    " Yet, did I mention this, I soon was told
That ' Conscience ' lacked development in such—
On some points 'twas developed ; not on all ;

34

THE VOICE OF THE OCEAN

'Twas this accounted for their going wrong.

  " On learning this, my mind (too logical)
Grew much affrighted of this Conscience-sense ;
If through such lack the savage went astray,
Then might not I ?　Who was to say I had
Such sense developed fully ?　If not, then
I might be daily erring in God's sight,
Though Mankind—part developed—knew it not.

  " And now, great Sea, can'st thou put me to rest ?
For I am so awearied with my doubts,
And more in earnest than the World might think."

Thus spake the Sea in answer to the soul :—

  " All knowledge is an ocean, and the drop
Gained by your wisest minds is small indeed ;
For ye are bound by bonds too visible,
Which blind ye to the path for gaining more.
  " Ye prate of right and wrong, and are but fools ;
Ye weep o'er things ye cannot understand,
And miss broad wisdom cast on every side,
Searching for that which never was nor is.
  " A thousand years ye have done wrong in vain,
And doing it ye hoped ye did some right :
Reason in your religions had no place,
Or if it had the place was out of sight.
  " I know that to do right is hard enough ;

35

THE VOICE OF THE OCEAN

But harder far when there are diff'rent views,
Holding that this is right, or that is wrong,
Without the intervention of hard sense.

   " They tell ye that to steal is wrong—and why ?
Because some ancient tablets said the same ;
Thus logic has small part in all their talk ;
'Tis logic that ye want to tell ye ' why.'

   " If someone said to some :—' 'Tis wrong to breathe,'
I wonder if that some would hold their breaths !
Yet 'tis the logic of most holy creeds ;
I do not wonder that ye pant for sense.

   " One stands upon a ladder, and he peers
Owlwise at stars ten-billion leagues away ;
Looks down with scorn from his small altitude,
And prates of things none at his feet can see !

   " He talks of many things in a sage voice ;
But cannot see past death to where life leaps,
Nor, on his drop of learning, sail beyond
The bar of death, which holds this life at bay.

   " The wise man with his ladder cannot pierce
Death's mystery ; nor anything but *guess !*
In matters so obscure he cannot see
One whit more deeply than his brothers do.

   " This being so, we must depend on Sense,
That strange and wondrous things, so common called,
Possessed in *some* degree by every soul ;
But used so little that it might not *be.*

36

THE VOICE OF THE OCEAN

" Now turn your thoughts about awhile, and think,
Perchance ye may find wisdom unawares ;
Ye want to know what's ' Right ' and what is ' Wrong,'
Methinks 'tis all the same as ' Good ' and ' Harm.'
    " For if ye work some ' Good ' to any soul
Ye may well claim to have done active ' Right ' ;
While if, on any, e'en small ' Harm ' ye work
'Tis just as certain you've done active ' Wrong.'
    " But if no ' Harm ' ye work in any wise
Ye certainly have done no active ' Wrong,'
Likewise, if guiltless ye of doing ' Good,'
Ye cannot be appraised for working ' Right.'
    " In later lives ye shall then bear the weight
Of all the ' Harm ' and ' Good ' ye e'er have worked,
And have ye done much active ' Good ' or ' Harm '
Your joys shall be the greater or the less.
    " Likewise, if ye live free from active ' Good,'
Equally so from working any ' Harm,'
Your bliss shall be not great, nor sorrow deep—
I wish ye joy in life so negative ! "

Thus ceased the Sea, and from the gloom about,
There came a song sung in a sleepy voice,
As though one sang while sleeping.

Thus it was :—

" There is no keen delight within that Place,

37

But rather lang'rous joy,
　　As though one looked across the World of
　　Sleep
And saw the dreamy face
　　Of the great soul of Peace rise from the deep
　　　Where slumberous dreams are born,
Far from the place where fears destroy,
　　Far from the place where morn
　　　Is but a messenger of tears and pain
　　　Destroying slumber's reign."

The Sea was quiet a moment ; then its voice,
Soft with an undernote of sympathy,
Came in a gentle song with promise filled :—

" Thou poor tired soul
　　(Who sing'st in dreams)
　　　With utter toil dismayed,
Comfort !　*Thy* goal—
　　The Deep of Rest—
Is nearer than it seems,
　　And there, though joy has been delayed,
　　Thou shalt an aeon sleep,
　　Waking, in dreams, to fuller zest
　　Of peace in that vast Deep."

Some timid moments fled, while silence reigned ;

38

THE VOICE OF THE OCEAN

Then from the night above, a voice swept down,
Filled in each tone with a poor soul's despair :—

" For all the years borne in the arms of Time
Shall not this burden ease, nor comfort me ;
Shall not upraise me from this dire despair.
No more the sky is blue—the sun shines not,
And my whole prayer is but to be forgot,
And in myself this dreariness forget
In death, where all shall be as though 'twere not ! "

Prompt was the Sea's reply :—

" Thou sorry soul,
It seems to me thou art too full of grief
To reason, or thou had'st not come to this.
" Doubtless, thou hast done wrong ; yet is this life
But one in many, and thou shalt have chance
To do some good, whereby thy harm shall be
Somewhat more balanced, though not blotted out ;
For a done wrong dies never ; 'twere as absurd
Almost as thinking cause had no effect ;
Yet, likewise, good dies never ; so thou shalt
Lay up in this, for future lives, some store
Of righteous deeds ; for in the Last Life thou
Shalt live eternally tremendous life
In the great culmination of thy deeds,

Both good and harmful ; therefore do thy best
Towards good deeds."

               A moment's quiet there was ;
Then cried that poor remorseful one in doubt :—

  " What are good deeds within the sight of God ?
No more than filthiest rags my mightiest good !
How shall these save my soul from lasting woe ?
How with my evil shall my good compare ?
I cannot hope to win to peace through deeds
That must, at best, sicken God's purity ! "

  No hesitation was there in reply :—

  " Thou must not think God reasonless—He has
Endowed thee with such powers as suit this state :
Thy righteousness, to His, may truly be
As filthy rags to a most glorious robe ;
But thou hast not God's strength, so trouble not,
And do remember that He is most just,
Expecting not of thee more than is meet :
So shall thy deeds of good count unto thee,
(Because of poor proficiency in right)
Equal, in this life, to much greater good
Worked in some future life of vaster power.
    " Calm thee, dear soul ! Now shake off thy remorse ;

THE VOICE OF THE OCEAN

Lose not one instant, but begin to live
As thou would'st live were each succeeding day
The last that thou would'st know.   Be comforted
In the hard work of doing good, spite of
Thy cross-grained human nature, which rebels
Against the will's authority, yet is
So diff'rent when well curbed and drawn by love.
   " Farewell awhile, O soul.   I may meet thee
In some far world, *working to happiness,*
Ah ! then how gladly shall my heart leap up ! "

   The Sea ceased from its speaking ; and at last,
My pent up feelings streamed abroad—I spoke :—

         " O, Sea !
         Listening to thee,
            I learn !
            I go beneath time's crust !
      We tread near on the life which is to be.
            Thy wisdom soothes my soul.   Thy sense is
               just !
      Thou hast no talk of hells which ever burn ;
            But that through many lives we are evolved
               By slow development (quick revolution
               slowed),
            Until all doubt, by preparation solved,
               Attain we to the Last Life—God's
               Abode."

THE VOICE OF THE OCEAN

The Sea was silent, and across the deeps
A gentle voice came softly, and began :—

" Lately, within my sleep, of future times,
Of the most future times this world shall know,
My dreams have been.
                              " I saw thee, O thou Sea,
'Mid the red loneliness of an evening's birth,
Wrapped in the quietude of an aching still.
    " Along thy shore I wandered, and my tears,
Born of thy silence, welled but could not fall.
    " I, who from out eternity had sped.
Only to look upon thy face once more,
Saw thy dead form ; for with this world, wert thou
Dead in the arms of Time, who once held me
Likewise when dead, ere I passed yonder, where,
Through a whole multitude of years, my dreams
Only had been of thee.
                              " And then, O, Sea,
E'en as I peered, through tears, across thy face,
I saw a movement in thy depths, as though
Thy life still stayed within thee ; then afar
I heard a sad, strange voice, despairingly
Come wailing o'er thy wastes.   And, O Great One !
'Twas full awhile ere I perceived 'twas thou
Whose dying voice sang o'er thy breathless plains,
Joining the awful gloom, whose palpitance

THE VOICE OF THE OCEAN

Of momentary blackness and anon of grey,
Pulsed nights and wintry dawnings o'er thy face.
  " And this long-cold, forgotten world, whose bulk,
Dying, but held thyself, its soul, O, Sea,
Echoed the sad'ning cadence of thy song—
The singing of thy dying voice, so that
In the last days of this old world thy voice,
Singing a song of agony 'mid gloom,
Came backward through the years unto my soul,
Pregnant with hopelessness and grief, until
It seemed to me that all the tears of life
Had spoken in thy song.
                    " That song, O, Sea,
With its sad rhythm, is past human tongue
To sing ; so I but conjure up its sense,
Though haltingly, and lacking all its power,
And all the sad'ning terror and the woe
Which trembled through its undertones, much as
A dirge moans ever in the lower notes
Of some cold, wintry gale o'er lonely shores :—

  " ' The world is dying, and I am alone,
In the deep silence, while the nearing sun
Belches an awful flare of lurid fire
Across the starkness of the dying world
And far across my almost silenced breast.
  " ' Done is my task of teaching life to men ;

43

THE VOICE OF THE OCEAN

No more the old emotions stir my soul ;
I am at peace, who ages was at war
With the great elements of strife that rose
And tortured me to fury in my youth.
Stilled is my anger in the long gone days ;
Steeped is my heart in tears in its deep place ;
Gone are the souls who loved me in the past,
And I am here alone—Oh ! so alone !
    " ' In a dim, far-off time, half-way between
The loneliness of two eternities,
I brood apart upon a dying world,
And pray that I were something more, or less,
Than what I am. For me there is no place
Beyond this place !
                " ' And now how I do feel
The pulsing of my heart at lowest ebb.
    " ' What is before me ? Who can tell ?—Not I !
Perhaps 'tis better that I do not know.

    " ' Even the mountains that upreared their crests
Upon my boundaries, have died, and now
They sleep upon the bosom of the world ;
And only my slow breathing on flat shores
Tells that the pulse of life is with me yet.
    " ' Now a great sense of cold oppresses me !
I wonder if this be indeed the end ;
Nay, surely not ; for God is great, and He

Shall do no less for me than other souls ;
And yet, 'tis strange how doubt creeps in when death
Draws nigh. 'Tis the great test. If faith survive,
In some new life I shall not need to shame.
" ' I will have faith, as I have always taught !
And yet, methinks if God were brought to die
He would have wondrous sympathy with me,
As, doubtless, now He has.
                " ' Ah ! colder still !
My God, who loved me in my youth and prime
Be with me now in this supremest test !
    " ' Haste thee now, Death !—'Tis such a natural
      fear !
And yet, I know thou dost but shore the sea
Of some tremendous life where holier thoughts
May keep the mind at peace. . . . Ah ! haste thee,
    Death ! '

  " Thus far I gat, and then a darkness came,
And thou wast hidden, and I was awake."

  Then ceased the voice, and in the furthest East
Shone the dear light of dawn, that emblem of
The dawn that crowns death's night. And from the
    West
There rose a sudden wind refreshingly,
That filled the air with hope, and murmured low
A message to the Sea from far beyond

THE VOICE OF THE OCEAN

The sudden gate of death.   And in the East
The tender lights still grew.
                          And afar the world
Reached up her sombre hills among the glow,
Into the pure, ethereal waters of
That sea of trembling hues which spumed and beat
Softly upon the shore of night, and surged
In beauteous sprays of foamy light above
The gloomy cliffs that edge the dayless shore,
And poured its living foam upon the world
In cataracts of light. . . .